The Effectual Church

Dr. Robert Louis Robinson

The Effectual Church

ISBN 9781724812902

To the believers who make of the kingdom of God

Table of Contents

The Demand

I wrote this book very quickly, with every chapter being written within a few hours. No excessive research was done, not many books or manuscripts were searched to balance the truth I am writing of. No, this book was written very fast and in season. The reason is that the Holy Spirit led me to write and release this book as soon as possible. This writing serves as a message to the body of Christ. God has placed a demand on the body of Christ. We have a mandate.

As I've stated in many of my writings, a mandate is an official order or commission to do something. Prophetically speaking, a kingdom mandate is the commission or order of the kingdom orchestrated by God. It is a set order which cannot be altered. Then there is the demand. What is a demand? Demand means to ask with authority. When God places a demand on your life, ministry, or the kingdom, it means He is asking us, with an authority, to move and move now. There is a reason behind the demand to the church; it's time for the church to come out of its hiding place and become the answer to the many questions the world has. The Body of Christ has a God-given mandate and He has placed a demand upon the church.

In my book *The Greater*, I stated "Time was created in eternity, time is used to govern God's purpose in the earth. Jesus said I must work the works of him while it is day or his hour. Time comes along with season." It is now the season of the church. What is meant by a season of the church? A season speaks of the situation created by God that calls for your time. If it's the season, then you know it's the church's time. Because it's the season of the church, God has literally placed a demand on the church which calls for the church's immediate attention or obedience.

Proverbs 10:22 reads, *"The blessing of the Lord, it maketh rich, and he addeth no sorrow with it."* This passage requires a little word study in order for you to get the message of the Demand on the Church. The word blessing is the Hebrew word *berakah* (ber-aw-kaw') which is derived from the Hebrew word *barak. Barak* means, "to bless, and to bend" which denotes a posture of worship. The word blessing *berakah* (ber-aw-kaw') in Proverbs 10:22 means, "To fill the palm" or "hand." The idea is to take something and place it inside of an individual. The blessing (*berakah*) or filling of the palm or hand is what the Lord has given the body of Christ. He has placed within the body of Christ that which is needed to be made rich. The word rich means to be made wealthy but it relates to a spiritual wealth. The Lord has filled the hands of the church with

2

that which makes the church spiritually wealthy. That blessing does not bring sorrow or grief, meaning the blessing produces a wealth within the body of Christ that will not bring any sorrow to those who are recipients of the display of the blessing. So then when functioning in the demand that God has placed upon the church, we the church operate in a blessing that releases sorrow from those who are recipients of the blessing.

Blessed is that servant, whom his lord when he cometh shall find so doing. Of a truth I say unto you, that he will make him ruler over all that he hath. But and if that servant say in his heart, My lord delayeth his coming; and shall begin to beat the menservants and maidens, and to eat and drink, and to be drunken; The lord of that servant will come in a day when he looketh not for him, and at an hour when he is not aware, and will cut him in sunder, and will appoint him his portion with the unbelievers. And that servant, which knew his lord's will, and prepared not himself, neither did according to his will, shall be beaten with many stripes. But he that knew not, and did commit things worthy of stripes, shall be beaten with few stripes. For unto whomsoever much is given, of him shall be much required: and to whom men have committed much, of him they will ask the more. (Luke 12:43-48)

To explain Luke 12:43-48, it focuses on a master and the obedience of his servant. When the master finds his servant working, it's a blessing to the servant because the

3

servant is chosen to take care of the master's property. The servant can become disobedient and when the master arrives to see that the servant is disobedient, the servant will be punished. This relates to the call of the Church, the call to those who are expected to know the will of God. They have been equipped with the will of God and looked upon to function within the will of God. I want to focus on the latter clause of verse 48: *"For unto whomsoever much is given, of him shall be much required: and to whom men have committed much, of him they will ask the more."* The word required is the Greek word *zeteo* (dzay-teh'-o), which means to look at something intently with desire for it to come forth. The Hebrew word for required is *baqash* (baw-kash') which means to search out—to intently look for someone or something until the object of the search is found. The Body of Christ has been given wealth as well as the understanding of what the Master wants out of the Church. To whom much is given, there must be a response to that which is given. That response is what is required from God. Because of the demand upon the church, there is an expectancy upon the church. To those who have committed much to the call of the kingdom, men will require out of you that which is expected of you. In other words, the demand and your obedience to the demand will call for men and women to seek you out because of that demand.

"Now the Lord had said unto Abram, Get thee out of thy country, and from thy kindred, and from thy father's house, unto a land that I will shew thee" (Genesis 12:1). Abram received two things; the first was a *dabar*. What is a *dabar*? The word *dabar* (daw-bawr') means an order or an arrangement of something creating order. It relates to a word of order or direction. Abram was ordered by God to leave or walk away from his father's house and go to a place where God will show him. Abram received a word of order that related to his future. The scripture reads that Abram departed Haran. The Hebrew word *Charan* (kaw-rawn') means parched; the root word means, "to melt, burn, dry up." Abram was told to leave the dry place. Haran was a place that would not be progressive even though it was the place of his inheritance. He wouldn't progress, so, the first thing Abram received was a *dabar,* a word of direction. Many of us today within the body is Christ are receiving a dabar, a word of direction. Some have been in a dry place of doing nothing for so long that it has become the norm. The demand is upon you and now God is waiting upon a response. To whom much is given, a response is required. Might I add, the greater the vision or demand, the greater the responsibility.

The second thing Abram received was a *neum*. What is a *neum*? Neum is a Hebrew word derived from the Hebrew word *naam,* which denotes an oracle. *Neum* denotes

5

a prophetic word declared through His prophets, which is the revelation of what God said. Abram received a prophetic word that dealt with his present situation at that time. *Dabar* brings you into your future; it's a word of direction. *Neum* deals with your now, where you are. Leave was a word for Abram's now, a *neum* which is what the Holy Spirit is speaking to the kingdom of God. We are receiving a *neum*, so leave where you are because it's not productive. You are burnt out on this level and there is much greater.

In my book entitled *Graced for Greatness*, I define those words as "A grace over one's life which enables them to progress, move forward, and move through and to finish their course." The kingdom of God is graced for greatness. We have been blessed to do the impossible. The demand has been placed upon the body of Christ and God is looking for the response which is required. Greatness speaks of doing the impossible through God; it speaks of the successful servant, the fight and progression within a servant. Because of the demand, we are equipped for the battle. Because of the mandate, we have no other alternative; we have no other choice—move forward and accomplish. Win over the world, break the spirit of deadness over the life of individuals, respond to a lost world. The *dabar* has been given, which relates to a word of order over your life. The *neum* has been given. God is dealing with your now; leave the place of mediocrity.

The Preacher

The term preacher in laymen's terms is one who delivers a sermon. In various situations such as a funeral, many identify the preacher because that individual is clothed in a collar, robe, or something that would identify him or her as one who delivers a sermon. In various religious settings, it seems a preacher can be singled out based upon what they wear and once that is noted, people already know what to expect. Many times, when I have preached a funeral and I am unknown, those attending know I'm the preacher because of what I wear. Traditionally then, the preacher is identified as an individual who wears certain religious clothing which identifies them and is traditionally known as the one who delivers a sermon.

1 Corinthians 12:28 reads, "And God hath set some in the church, first apostles, secondarily prophets, thirdly teachers, after that miracles, then gifts of healings, helps, governments, diversities of tongues." The first portion of the text focuses on the gifts God has set in the church which are first apostles, secondarily prophets, thirdly teachers. The apostle governs the sheep, the prophet guides the sheep, while the teacher grounds the sheep. Sheep refers to believers within the body of Christ. After the gifts are noted in 1 Corinthians, then the ministry of

the Church is noted. What is meant by the term ministry of the church? It notes what the church as a whole brings to a lost world; it's the ministry that the church offers, which is the ability of supernatural works or gift of healings, which is the endowment from God that makes the church able to bring healing or a cure. The ministry of helps brings relief while the ministry of government brings balance. The diversity of tongues is the ministry of the church that gives the ability to minister or serve every nation with no hindrance of languages. The church will supernaturally speak every language of the world. These are the ministries the church functions in.[1]

The church is the response to a lost world. The church as a whole does bring something to the table, we bring a healing to every situation that the world is facing. I believe in some cases that tradition can kill a remedy. Meaning, if someone is sick but traditionally they are afraid of doctors, they rule out or even kill their remedy which is their means to get better. That is the same in ministry; tradition can sometimes kill a remedy. Mark 7:13 reads: "Making the word of God of none effect through your tradition, which ye have delivered: and many

---

[1] Robinson, Robert. The Mighty Hand of the Lord. Cranston, RI: DaveDez Publishing, 2015

such like things do ye." Jesus was saying you honor tradition above honoring what God said. Tradition has a tendency to kill the remedy. Traditional thinking will rule out revelation. The traditional thinking that the preacher should have on a collar, robe, or suit limit preaching!

Remember, the ministry of the church is the response to the world. The ministry of the church is done through the preaching. A very seasoned Man of God told me years ago, you do not teach the Bible to the world; you preach to the world, you teach the church. So, it is important to understand how important it is to preach to the world. The response to a troubled world is the Church, the Body of Christ. How does the church respond? The church responds through preaching.

I know that many who are reading this are wondering what in the world is Dr. Robinson talking about? But let's look at the scriptures.

For whosoever shall call upon the name of the Lord shall be saved. How then shall they call on him in whom they have not believed? and how shall they believe in him of whom they have not heard? and how shall they hear without a preacher? And how shall they preach, except they be sent? as it is written, How beautiful are the feet of them that preach the gospel of peace, and bring glad tidings of good things! (Romans 10:13-15)

For whosoever shall call upon the name of the Lord shall be saved. The word saved is the Greek word *sozo* (*sode'-zo*); the root word is *saos* which means safe. This word *sozo* means delivered, protected, healed, preserved, made whole. The Hebrew word for save is *yasha* (*yaw-shah'*) which means rescue, to be free or deliver from a trouble, burden or danger. Whosoever calls upon the name of the Lord shall be rescued and delivered. The scripture goes on then to ask a question: how then shall they call on Him in whom they have not believed, and how shall they believe in him of whom they have not heard? In other words, how can they call upon the name of the Lord if they don't believe in the name because they have not heard of the name? Understand that there is a remedy to the world's spiritual sickness but if the world is not made aware of the remedy, then traditionally the world will continue to think and believe they are lost.

The middleman between the world and the church is the preacher. Note what the scripture says, how shall they hear without a preacher, and how shall they preach except they be sent? First, let's look at the word preacher from a biblical standpoint and not the traditional view. The word preacher is the Greek word *kerusso* (kay-roos'-so), which means to herald or to announce; *kerusso* refers to a public crier, especially of divine truth. But it goes deeper than that. The preacher, heralder, or announcer of divine truth is sent or dispatched to a place and are dispatched to a place with the remedy. My question is how does the preacher preach? You preach by expressing who Jesus is in a form that God has given you. Preaching is the means the church has to win over a lost world. But how do you preach, how do you project Jesus? Jesus preaching is projected through your uniqueness. Your gifting is your uniqueness which causes you to project Jesus in a unique way. That unique way catches the ears of those who hear. The preacher is the individual who has an anointing upon their life that reveals Jesus in a unique and might I say non-traditional way.

How can the preacher preach except they be sent? The word sent has two types of meanings. The Greek word *pempo* (*pem'-po*) means to dispatch from a departure point to arrive at the place sent on a temporary basis, to be sent on an errand temporarily. In Acts 10:17, 20, God commanded Cornelius to send (pempo) for Simon Peter. Pempo means "to do one a favor and go on an errand temporarily, go and fetch." *Pempo* requires obedience. The second word for sent which is noted here in Romans 10:15, is *apostello* (*ap-os-tel'-lo*) This word means set apart as to send away. It implies that one is sent out to a place, one being sent on an assignment. How can they preach except they be sent? Some are sent as a *pempo* (temporary assignment, errand) and some are sent to place for a long-term assignment. The situation requires that you preach, which calls for a display of your uniqueness. That display of uniqueness is anointed by the Holy Spirit which will, in turn, release the ministry of the church which touches every need an individual has.

In our church, House of Manna Ministries, we have a dance team that was well known for their unique way of dancing. Traditionally, the type of dancing would not have been accepted in the church I grew up in because it would have been viewed as "too much like the world." I've noticed through the years with the dance team that it was their expression, it was how they preached, they displayed Jesus through the movement of their bodies. I remember one time in particular I was doing a crusade in Waterbury Connecticut. The park we were using was surrounded by a basketball court and there was many at the basketball court. As we started singing, very few would come over and watch. Some would sing along with us and get involved; however, those that were at the basketball court continued to play basketball. Before I got up to minister, we called for the dance team to minister. They took their place on stage and they started with the music, loudly. However, those playing basketball in the courts, once they heard the music, stopped playing. They left the basketball court and came over to the meeting. They watched, they were moving and swaying, and they enjoyed

14

what they saw. Many have been blessed by the dance team. It took traditional me to realize that preaching is not only done from behind a pulpit. Preaching is done in action; it's how you project Jesus, that is the preaching.

We have had young people come to our ministry because of the dance team. My son David (who's never studied dancing) is responsible for teaching many how to dance. Some had no belief in themselves, but he worked on their confidence and taught them. They projected Jesus, they preached Jesus through dance. Again, it's how you project Jesus that determines the preaching.

Years ago, in my city, there was a terrible house fire in which people died. There was a church mother who was looking at the house and while she was there, she noticed a young lady crying profusely. The young lady was hurt and angry and so when the mother reached out to the young lady, she snapped at the mother. She told the mother to leave her alone, get away, she doesn't believe in that Jesus junk. But the Mother kept preaching to her. No there was no pulpit, the Church mother had no preachers license, the church mother did not have a degree in theology. The church mother did not have music, did not have a choir to entertain the young lady. There was no one there but police, rescue a burning house, sadness, bewilderment, hurt, and anger.

Mother continued to talk to the young lady. In her own way, she preached to the young lady. A few moments later, the mother was seen holding the young lady who was weeping in mother's arms. The young lady not only heard the message of Christ but embraced it. It didn't happen in a church, but it did happen in a terrible situation. Yes, the situation was a house fire where lives were lost; however, for the young lady, the church had a remedy. Tradition wasn't the remedy; preaching was. The preaching from the church mother was unique. It came through the humble loving spirit of that mother who acted as a mother to win the young lady over. Remember, whosoever calls upon the name of the Lord shall be saved.

How can they hear without the preacher and how can they preach except they be sent on assignment or an errand? Many believers have forsaken their assignments of preaching because it was not based upon their traditional way of preaching. I can hear many of you saying "I'm no preacher," but I beg to differ. When it comes down to expanding the kingdom of God and bringing hope to many, yes, my brother and sister, you are a preacher. Not in the traditional sense but you are called to uniquely project who Jesus is. My prayer is that God be glorified through your preaching.

The Faith that it Takes

In all that we do within the kingdom of God to win a lost world, it will require faith. In regard to the subject of faith, there are many facets to faith, yet faith is the most powerful weapon the church has while functioning in this world system. It is then important to understand that there are many facets to faith. In this chapter, we will look at three facets of faith. The first being noted in 2 Timothy 4:7.

In 2 Timothy 4:7, Paul the Apostle states, "*I have fought a good fight, I have finished my course, I have kept the faith.*" The words that are given in the text are extremely important and require word-study on a few of them. The words "I have" are in the perfect tense of a Greek verb which relates to a struggle that was bravely sustained in the past and is now being equally bravely sustained to the end. Paul is saying, based upon what I've been through and was sustained in the time past, I now have the confidence that I am being sustained even now. His confidence in being sustained is based upon his past experiences. The idea is that Paul is confident that he has fought a good fight.

The term "I have fought a good fight" is not the proper translation. It should read, I have fought "the good fight." The word fight is the Greek word *agon* (ag-one') which denotes being led to a place of assembly that contains a contest, effort, or conflict. To this point, we are understanding that Paul is confident based on past experiences that he has fought the good fight or conflict presented before him. The word finished is the Greek word *teleo* (tel-eh'-o), which is taken from the Greek word *tello,* which means to set out for a goal. *Teleo* means to complete, execute, conclude, discharge a debt. *Teleo* literally means to set out and complete, to pay the debt. Paul through his experiences has come to the conclusion that he fought the good contest which he was led into and completed.

Still looking at 2 Timothy 4:7, we will focus on the last words of that verse which will teach us a facet of faith. The words to focus on are *"I have kept the faith."* What does the term "I have kept the faith" mean? It means that against all types of persuasions and influences, Paul has maintained the faith of the Gospel. What is his faith of the gospel? Paul's faith of the gospel is his confession that Jesus Christ is the Messiah. The confession that Paul maintained is the type of faith the church of God must maintain and that is we believe Jesus is the Christ. When you have kept "The Faith" against all obstacles and influences, you have kept your belief in Jesus who is the object of our faith.

Paul is confident based on past experiences and he has fought the good fight. He has completed his journey (he paid the debt) and he has held on to his belief in Jesus in that Jesus is the Christ. He's had many influences, but he never stopped believing and left the faith. So, maintaining your faith in God is a facet of faith. The church of God must never lose focus on who Jesus is—He is the object of our faith.

Another facet of faith is an act of obedience, noted in Hebrews 11:4-8.

By faith Abel offered unto God a more excellent sacrifice than Cain, by which he obtained witness that he was righteous, God testifying of his gifts: and by it he being dead yet speaketh. (5) By faith Enoch was translated that he should not see death; and was not found, because God had translated him: for before his translation he had this testimony, that he pleased God. (6) But without faith it is impossible to please him: for he that cometh to God must believe that he is, and that he is a rewarder of them that diligently seek him. (7) By faith Noah, being warned of God of things not seen as yet, moved with fear, prepared an ark to the saving of his house; by the which he condemned the world, and became heir of the righteousness which is by faith. (8) By faith Abraham, when he was called to go out into a place which he should after receive for an inheritance, obeyed; and he went out, not knowing whither he went. (Heb. 11:4-8)

In Hebrews 11: 4-8, there are noted acts of faith or actions of faith which happened because of their obedience. Acts of faith are also actions of obedience. Note the examples from Hebrews 11:4-8:

- In Heb. 11:4, we note Abel offered unto God a more excellent sacrifice than Cain. It was his act of obedience which was an action of faith.
- In Heb. 11:5, Enoch was translated that he should not see death and was not found, because God had translated him: for before his translation he had this testimony, that he pleased God. An act of obedience which was an action of faith.
- In Heb. 4:7, Noah being warned by God of things not seen as yet, moved with fear, prepared an ark to the saving of his house. It was his act of obedience which was an action of faith.
- In Heb. 11:8, Abraham when he was called to go out of a place which he should receive for an inheritance, obeyed. It was

his act of obedience which was an action of faith.

A good friend of mine taught that there is something greater than your worship and that is obedience. 1st Samuel 15:22 reads, *"Behold, to obey is better than sacrifice."* One of the Hebrew words for obedience is *shama`* (shaw-mah') which means, "To hear intelligently and attentively and respond appropriately." Hearing God is one point of obedience while responding appropriately is the action of faith. It denotes you, believer, hearing then carrying out what you have heard. Obedience is the highest praise and the highest level of worship one can offer unto the Lord; it is the highest act of faith one can offer. Hebrews 11:4-8 reveals examples of obedience which led to action of faith; they heard and then they carried it out.

One facet of faith speaks of the faith that is our foundation. It's our confession of what we believe and who we believe in—Jesus the Christ, the Son of the Living God. The second facet of faith is obedience to God, which reveals actions of faith.

Thirdly, we will look at a final facet of faith called persistence and warfare. It is the passion and the driving force of the church's purpose. When you operate in faith, usually it's an operation that goes against all odds, so it is an act of persistence and warfare. I've said that faith is the possibility of the impossibility; it causes the impossible to be possible. In order for faith to do that which it does, then faith is both persistence and warfare, operating in faith is warfare. A persistent and warfare faith depends totally on God. It is divinely revealed, divinely supported, and miraculously revealed which produces results.

In Hebrews 11:30-32 there is to note beautiful examples of warfare that are noted by or because of faith (persistence and warfare). In verse 30, by faith the walls of Jericho fell down after they were compassed about seven days. Why did the walls fall? Because of the obedience and their persistence. Their persistence was a type of warfare that stated we are not quitting and are fighting against the odds. In verse 31, Rahab through her act of faith saved the spies of the church which resulted in her peace. Her acts of faith were the result of her obedience which speaks of the persistence and warfare of those who believe in vision. They take part in what the vision is and bless it by doing their part. Note Hebrews 11:32: "And what shall I more say? for the time would fail me to tell of Gedeon, and *of* Barak, and *of* Samson, and *of* Jephthae; *of* David also, and Samuel, and *of* the prophets." What were their accomplishments? Gedeon destroyed an army with only 300 (Judges 6, 7, 8.). Barak was summoned by Deborah to make war against Jabin who held the Israelites as slaves for many years. Against all odds, Barak defeated Jabin and delivered Israel from slavery (Judges 4). Samson delivered Israel from the oppressive Philistines (Judges 13-16). Jephthae, whose name means "whom God sets free or the breaker through" against all odds, defeated the Ammonites and delivered Israel. Jephthae believed in the promise made to Abraham and that they should possess the land of Canaan (Judges 11; 12:1-15). Against all odds, a young man named David slew Goliath, an intimidating giant who oppressed the chosen Children of Israel. There, faith was on display based upon their obedience and they were driven to a point where a response was needed. Operating in faith is how the Church of God responds to an intimidating situation presented by the enemy.

Hebrews 11:33 reads, *"Who through faith subdued kingdoms, wrought righteousness, obtained promises, stopped the mouths of lions."* I want to look at a word there which is extremely important. The word subdued requires examination. Subdued is the Greek word *katagonizomai* (kat-ag-o-nid'-zom-ahee), which means to struggle against but overcome. My point is, subdued teaches us that the battle was just a walk through the park. It was going to be tough; they had to fight, struggle but they had the mentality that they were going to overcome. Remember the third facet of faith we are discussing is persistence and warfare. When they subdued kingdoms, it took persistence and definitely warfare because the enemy was not going to just give in.

The examples of walks of faith or demonstrations of faith being seen in many was not always a pretty thing to see. Many suffered for the faith. Cruel mockings and scourgings relate to what Paul said regarding him keeping the faith. Against all odds and persuasions, the trial of cruel mockings and scourgings did not cause the believers to relinquish their faith and belief in their confession. They all obtained a good report through faith. The effectual church has the faith that it takes in order to move and complete a kingdom agenda in the earth.

The Effectual Church

From whom the whole body fitly joined together and compacted by that which every joint supplieth, according to the effectual working in the measure of every part, maketh increase of the body unto the edifying of itself in love. (Eph. 4:16)

In Ephesians 4:16, the whole body is fitly joined together meaning the body is compacted or driven together. The body in Ephesians 4:16 is referring to the body of Christ. It is fitly or laid close together; each body part serves its own purpose to cause His body to function according to the effectual working. What is meant by the word effectual? The word effectual is the Greek word *energeia* (en-erg'-i-ah) from which we get the English word energy. It means strong, working operation. The body of Christ then is formed together in order to produce a strong working operation. No part of the body is greater than the other, for each has its own job. The task within the body is causing the Light and Life of Christ to shine in a dark world and this body is who I refer to as the Effectual Church.

The Effectual Church is a functioning group of people from all walks of life called and appointed by God to bring a difference. This body is a group of believers created for adversity in order to bring salvation to a world that is lost.

When Israel went out of Egypt, the house of Jacob from a people of strange language; Judah was his sanctuary, and Israel his dominion. The sea saw it, and fled: Jordan was driven back. The mountains skipped like rams, and the little hills like lambs. (Ps. 114:1-4)

Note that when Israel left Egypt or pulled away from the bondage they were in, Judah became His sanctuary and Israel His dominion. In other words, Judah became His *qodesh* (ko'-desh) meaning His sacred place, a holy thing, a place set aside for the purpose of the glory of the Lord to be shown. The Bible goes on to read that Israel became his dominion *memshalah* (mem-shaw-law') which means authority, power to rule. Both words Judah and Israel represent His reign within His people. So, then the effectual church in the midst of it is the reign of God who lives in the midst of His people who are His sanctuary.

Psalms 114 reads that, the sea saw it, the river Jordan was driven back, the mountains skipped like rams and the hills like lambs. This speaks of the dominion of the kingdom which reveals and effectual church in the earth. Since the church has that much dominance and command in the earth there is nothing the church cannot face. The effectual church is a group that is not hindered by the world system but brings answers to that system.

As previously stated, God has placed a demand on the Church. It is a demand that requires the church to move forward, take dominion, be a voice of hope, and be about the demonstration of the spirit of God. When the church as a whole becomes about the demonstration of the spirit of God, that is when the church becomes the preacher and in its unique way, presents Jesus to the world through a means that could be identified with the now.

The effectual church is a group of believers who operates in the three facets of faith—their belief, their obedience, and their persistence and warfare. Faith in Him is our foundation, faith and obedience is our service, persistence and warfare of faith is the effectual church's weapon. Faith is the means of operation that the effectual church gets things done, faith causes the impossible to become possible. This is the effectual church. This is the group of believers that will be effective in a dark world who feels that all hope is lost.

Books by Dr. Robinson

Can These Bones Live?
A writing based on the book of Ezekiel 37:1-14.

An Appointed Time
An encouragement to those who have been sidelined by the works of the enemy.

The Authority of the Kingdom
This writing serves as a wakeup call to all believers in regard to what the Father has invested in the kingdom

Build Me A House
A motivational prophetic Word based on the book of Ezra.

Build Me A House Correspondence Course
Correspondence Course based on the book entitled "Build Me A House."

Hebrews Chapter Nine "The Interpretation"
A verse by verse commentary on the ninth chapter of the book of Hebrews.

Lessons I've Learned
This book is a compilation of bible studies taught by Dr. Robinson.

House of Manna Ministries International Leadership Manual
Operations manual for House of Manna Ministries. Will assist other ministries in establishing balanced leadership within the local assembly

The Necessity for Leadership
This book deals with the need and importance of spiritual leadership.

His Praise
This book teaches of the Hebrew Praise Words.

A Sevenfold Purpose w/workbook
The Sevenfold Purpose is the revealing of the will of God to His church as it pertains to alignment and order.

The Numbers Revealed
A prophetic view concerning numbers throughout the Bible

How we got the Bible
This book gives information concerning the history and makeup of the Bible. It deals with the many testing that were done in order to prove its authenticity.

How we got the Bible Workbook

Revelation, The Book
A commentary of the New Testament prophetical book of Revelations.

Revelation, The Book Workbook
This is the workbook to "Revelation the Book."

The Ministry of the Tabernacle
This book is gives detailed information on the Tabernacle of Moses. This book includes the work book

The Ministry of the Tabernacle Workbook
The Workbook to the book The Ministry of the Tabernacle.

A Survey of the Old Testament
This book focuses on the Old Testament and deals with the History of Israel, their Kings, prophets, priests and ordinances.

A Survey of the Old Testament Workbook
The workbook to A survey of the Old Testament

Words Defined Prophetically
A book containing a selection of Biblical, Hebrew and Greek words detailing information concerning their meaning.

A Time to Work
This book serves as a word to believers concerning a period when God will release an anointing for seed and harvest

The Authority of the Kingdom
A wakeup call to all believers in regard to what the Father has invested in the kingdom.

The Four Anointing's
A prophetical writing on the four rivers noted in Genesis chapter 3

What are you Birthing?
This writing is based upon the book of Luke concerning the father of John the Baptist names Zacharias.

Vision, "The Pattern"
Vision is a book that goes into detail concerning vision and how to manifest vision.

Vision, "The Pattern" Workbook
The Workbook to "Vision the Pattern"

Hebraic and Prophetic Interpretation of Biblical Words of the Old Testament
Definitions of words of the Old Testament

Feasts of the Lord
The Feasts of the Lord is a prophetic look at the Old Testament Feast Days

Let's Get It Done!
This book serves as a charge to all believers to get the work of the Lord completed. Time is of the essence

Let's Get It Done Workbook

Embrace the Transition
This book ministers to those going through a time of transition for the sake of the kingdom

New Testament Survey
This book gives a brief synopsis of all New Testament books. Book also contains question and answers.

Your Assignment
This book encourages the believer to stay focused on what God has entrusted to them, their assignment.

The Hand of the Lord
A Teaching on the Fivefold Ministry

The Eulogy
God the Father has blessed the believer with a good word over the life of the believer

Principles for Purpose
Principles on how one should focus and handle their purpose

Spiritual Laws
This book gives information regarding the rights of the believer

Jude's Letter
This is a writing based upon the book of Jude. In it you will find that Jude not only wrote to his generation, but his writings are prophetic which allowed for those writings to also speak to this generation.

11084542R10023

Made in the USA
Lexington, KY
11 October 2018